I CAN ONLY OFFER
YOU EVERYTHING

I CAN ONLY OFFER YOU EVERYTHING

poetry and prose

kelsey kasischke

ISBN-13: 979-8-9912315-3-4
First Edition, June 2025

Cover designed by Kelsey Kasischke
Cover graphic designed by Nina, Adobe File ID #576256590

DEDICATION

For the girl I was, and the woman I'm becoming.

For the family and friends who've supported me and my
writing every step of the way.

And for the reader who thinks like me, feels like me, falls
like me, dreams like me- I hope you find a little bit of
yourself somewhere in these pages.

contents

introduction...........................9

sincerity..............................13

alchemy...............................35

verity.................................57

reverie................................85

about the author..................112

There's an ineloquence of sorts
to any love that rings true.

Kelsey Kasischke

INTRODUCTION

There's an ineloquence of sorts to any love that rings true.

It's the requisite disarray of a heart lain bare- a beautiful mess of disheveled adoration and trembling bravado, brutally exposed and yet, somehow, safe. It's a vulnerability that can't help but bear the evidence of those that failed to handle it gently, the sacred remains of past lives in ruins.

It's an unbound and unbridled state of grace, a quintessential coexistence of soft and shameless. It's sincerity and verity, alchemy and reverie, all so messily immaculate, all so *ineloquent*.

And so it must be- to see and be seen, to know and be known, love and be loved.

I think ineloquent love throws its head back laughing at the dinner table and wipes away tears in the second stall. I think it shows up without warning, without makeup, without the table made or the counters cleaned. I think its voice shakes and its tongue ties and its heart slips from its sleeve with or without its permission.

I think it strips down, lays bare, revives and unbinds, I think it stutters and stalls till it finds its mark, I think it swallows all sense and semblance of pride, and I think it makes a haven of even the hollowest of hearts.

I've kissed a boy at a Speedway station in Cleveland and I've held myself together on cold kitchen tile. I've fallen head over first-date heels in a Kroger parking lot and, four months later, fallen to pieces in another. I've picked out a dress for a *friend's* new flame and masqueraded a smile at the party, worn out "*you two are great together*" and tried, God, *tried*, to mean it.

I've overpacked and underprepared, stifled the knot in my stomach and booked the flight for the sake of showing up, of *being there*. I've been lost in a college town and lost in cities abroad, lost in my own little world and in petrified wonder at just how big this world really is. I've cracked a smile, albeit broken, for the mosaic in the mirror more times than I can count.

I've cried over the kindness of strangers and I've wept watching friends become them. I've held myself through nightmares and held calloused hands, coded *I love you* in countless tongues and scribbled it into years worth of semi-poetic prose.

I've looked too long and I've tried too hard, lived and, at long last, learned that **to love is to let yourself go.**

To say *I love you* in any way you know how.

Ineloquent as it may be.

Because I cannot, will not,
produce something halfhearted
from a heart that loves wholly, or not at all.

Kelsey Kasischke

SINCERITY

We were the inevitability that never was.

We were shadows and satellites:
one never far behind the other,
always in orbit but never colliding,
always on the tips of our toes,
never making it past the tips of our tongues.

We were a lone tightrope lap around the sun—
four seasons spent skirting subjects and sparking rumors,
holding on and out,
raising eyebrows and questions,
questions the two of us were asked by **everyone except each other.**

I still wonder if your answers sounded anything like mine.

I *told* you.

I told you in questions and conversation,
glances and grapevines
prayers and pining and patience
In songs and stories,
favors and flushed cheeks,
lyrics and laughter and long looks

I told you in breadcrumbs and blind hope,
changes of subject and changes of plans,
expressions I couldn't hide and questions I couldn't ask
In taking your lead and taking your time,
not-so-random chances and not-so-false rumors

Then,

In a fallen face and sunken shoulders
the night my house of cards finally came crashing down
In the solo walk home I spent counting cracks in the sidewalk,
heavy with the nine month wait
trailing my footsteps like a ball and chain

In realizing that I wanted you to be happy
more than I needed to be the reason,
and in walking away when you found your reason.

No, it never passed through my lips;
all that time, and the words never left the tip of my tongue.

But don't you dare say I never told you.

You always asked why I never wrote about you.

As if I hadn't,
as if you didn't know me well enough to know
that I'd written about you a million times in my mind,
just never out loud,
never in a way that would allow me to see it all spelled out,
that would require me to read it and wonder
if the writer knew just how ignorant she sounded,
if she was really blind or just blindfolded,
dumb or in denial,
and *I wonder if it ever occurred to you*
that I could not write down what I was not prepared to read.

Because the fact is that you made a companion
of a girl conditioned to know platonic love as a placeholder
and a pair like us as a perishable good,
and the moment I realized you were my best friend
is the very moment the panic took root
because you have to understand that
nobody with that title has ever stayed their welcome.

You have to understand
that these are the very things I never learned to hold onto,
that *these are the losses that have branded me*
far longer than any flame I've ever held.

And the truth is that the version of us we'd accepted
always felt like a placeholder,
an interim means to an inevitable ending,
be it happy or otherwise.

Because people like us can be friends, sure-
    but friends like us cannot stay friends.

Friends like us don't give speeches at each other's weddings;
    they meet at the altar or get scratched from the guest list.

And I have to think you knew it too:
that something had to give,
that it could only be as it was until it wasn't,
that from the moment this thing
found its footing and started to matter
we were on a fast-track to a fork in the road

And I think you knew it too,
that at some point up ahead there would be no staying put,
no leaving the way we came-

    that at some point we would be each other's to love or to lose.

By the time I got there, you were already gone.

Moderation is not a friend of mine.

I have never known nonchalance,
never had a taste for lukewarm or half-baked;
I like my music roaring and my mornings silent,
my goals exceeded and ambiguity exiled,
my heart loved or left alone.

Either I remain on shore,
both feet planted firmly in the ground,
or I *dive-*
I do not know how to tread water on the surface of inspiration,
and I do not care to know;
because my greatest strength
lies in my capacity to be captivated,
the most moving thing about me
is my willingness to be moved.

This is not to say that I pour out readily, recklessly-
no, *I cannot afford to;*
Because what's within my walls
could fill canyons to the brim,
could submerge cities and move mountains,
could change the landscape of your world as well as mine-
so do not reach up and open the floodgates if you are not prepared to swim.

Because I cannot, will not,
produce something halfhearted
from a heart that loves wholly, or not at all.

-Forgive me,

I can only offer you everything.

My learning to love me
has been an endeavor far too central to my story
for me to entertain the thought of begging to be loved
by someone who has no intention of doing it well.

My vow to take care of me
has been a commitment much too long in the making
for me to consider handing my heart
to someone with no desire to hold it gently.

Because I have not always had an ally in this self of mine.

But now?

Now I will fight to keep her, even if you won't.

Now I will choose her, even if you don't.

Now I will not let me lose me-

even if you will.

All of that,
only for me to lose the one
for whom I would have gone to hell and back
in half of a heartbeat-
one who, when all was said and done,
ended up being the one to put me through it.

You made a fool of me, no doubt.

And all of that,
only for you to lose someone
who believed in you relentlessly,
defended you adamantly,
trusted you wholeheartedly.

You made a fool of you too.

I believed in you relentlessly.

My faith in you was unwavering,
unshaken even through every fall from grace
I blamed expectations, timing,
miscommunication and misunderstandings,
blamed anything and anyone but you,
then blamed myself when I ran out of fingers to point.

What a fool.

The truth is, I never so much as considered
the possibility of you letting me down
until I couldn't sink any further,
didn't feel you clipping my wings until I hit the pavement,
had no idea that you'd cut me down
until I looked up to find you worlds away
and could hardly recall how we used to stand side by side.

What a fool.

All of that, only for me to lose the one
for whom I would have gone to hell and back
in half of a heartbeat-
one who, when all was said and done,
ended up being the one to put me through it.

What a fool.

And all of that, only for you to lose the one
who believed in you relentlessly,
defended you adamantly,
trusted you wholeheartedly-

What a fool.

I used to pray for you every night.

It was like clockwork,
habitual,
my way of bidding farewell to every day:
by asking politely to find you in the next one.

I did it through the good days and the bad,

from the ones I spent skipping across cloud nine,
to the night the floor fell through;
the ones I spent spinning around in a parking lot,
feet lifted off the ground,
to the time I woke to the feeling of pavement on my skin,
kneeling on bruised knees to send up the same tired prayer

Because I did it through the good days and the bad,

night after night,
and every single one of them ended with the same six words:

Please don't let me lose him.

For what it's worth,
I still pray for you.

But my prayers end a little differently these days.

A silent assassin is no less a killer.

You know that, right?

You're no less guilty for never having said goodbye.

I have felt undeserving before and survived it,
though not without striving, without pain

but I would venture to say that
to be *undeserved* by the one you want
is excruciating to an entirely new degree.

But that's the way it works, isn't it?

When something dies
you never receive the news from the dearly departed-
no, you only hear it from the witnesses,
the loved and left behind

That's why denial runs rampant when the casket is closed.

That's why it took me so long to stop trying to pry ours open.

To believe them when they told me there was nothing left to save.

And I don't know why the sunshine makes me nostalgic

but I'm lying in a backyard in Carolina
and before I know it
I'm poolside in Cincy
writing letters to a lost cause
same green bikini, different plans
same blue above me, different shade within

Then the pass of a cloud
and I'm oceanside in Port Saint Joe,
same heart, different hurt,
same eyes dripping saltwater on the sand
now trailing little rivulets under a palmetto state sky, and *God*
I don't remember when I last went down this road,
but it's changed since I last drove it:
a little sweeter, less bitter
different state, different mind.

And I don't know why the sunshine makes me nostalgic
but I'm lying in a backyard in Carolina
and it's burning my eyelids and healing somehow
and **I guess all I'm trying to say** is that
somewhere, someway,
whoever you've become and whatever you wish for me now,

I hope it's shining on you too.

I am twenty-five years old,
and I think I've fallen in love for the last time.

    I think the adrenaline's already lost its allure,
    wilted one too many times into soul-wrenching withdrawal
    I suppose I peered behind the curtain and walked away jaded,
    saw the subtle masochism in the so-called magic
    and at last confronted the flip-side of the facade:

    The fall is never free.

It was a price I was willing to pay, once.

    I spent my days chasing sparks,
    savored the taste of danger,
    craved the kind of love that detonates
    I stifled the slow burn and swore off the safe play,
    staked my heart on a head rush and made my bed in oblivion
    only to crash on the comedown like a lovesick Icarus,
    asphalt plastered to my empty palms

And so I've fallen for the last time,
thank God.

    Because now I'm twenty-something on a Tuesday night,
    crinkling the corners of the kindest eyes mine have ever known,
    gentle hands of *just a friend* reaching for mine in a brand new way
    and I'm starting to think that maybe it's better when it blossoms,
    beautiful to build it from the ground up.

And I cannot say whether we'll end up in love,
but wherever we're going, we're going hand-in-hand.

Wherever we're going,

I've never been more content to take the long way.

And if I should wake from wildest dreams to know I'll never hold him,

I pray at least to thank him for the gray days he made golden.

You gave me something to look forward to, however ordinary;

A *good morning* waiting for me when I woke,
an *I'll be there soon* or *I'll see you tomorrow*,
all those weekend plans and someday dreams

Don't you see it?

You gave me a reason to lift my eyes
from the ground beneath my feet
for the first time in a long time,
gave me hope for a tomorrow I had ceased to believe in

You gave me something to look forward to
when I'd long been too afraid to look forward at all.

Thank you will never be enough.

I could tell you until I'm blue in the face
that I never want to change you,
and every time it would be a lie.

To be loved at all is to be changed.

The essence should stay, but the restless must go,
the wild remain but the running meet its end
The heart in your chest should stay fierce and stay true,
its beat stronger with another life to live for

If the imprints of your storyline before and after my arrival
do not look like either side of a revival, an awakening,
I dare say neither of us are where we belong.

Yes, I could tell you that I never want my love to change you,
to make waves,
to interrupt or intrude
on any aspect of your world as you know it,
but that couldn't be further from the truth-

*I want it to alter the very flight of the stars
until the constellations themselves letter our names.*

How do I tell him?

> That the reason
> no one came to the door when he knocked
> was that I could not, for the life of me,
> find my way home

> That the reason
> no one reached for his outstretched hand
> was that I was far too busy living in my head
> to be in my body

How do I tell him?

> These days there's a light on the porch,
> a pot on the stove.

> A *sorry* on the tip of my tongue.

Is it too late to tell him?

> **I'm back in my body now.**

> I'm back,

> I'm back,

> *come back.*

I leave you feeling like I've left something behind.

Like-
walking away from you
is wading upstream,
leaving my own little corner of Eden,
trying to fall towards the sky

That's always how it starts, isn't it?

Little by little,
     brick by brick,
          you begin to make a home in another human.

Little by little,
     long before they're yours,
          love takes root in this insatiable instinct,

               this pocket-sized impulse to *stay*.

Everyone I have ever loved, whether here or gone,
now carries a piece of me with them wherever they go.

This always has been, and always will be, true.

But tonight, for the first time,
I wonder how many people
have likewise given me pieces of themselves
that they never got back.

Tonight I wonder how many people have,
with or without my knowing,
entrusted me with parts of themselves
that they knew might never be fully theirs ever again.

I wonder if they believe they're in good hands.

I wonder if they know that I am honored to hold them.

There are parts of my story I pray you never understand.

Kelsey Kasischke

ALCHEMY

There are parts of my story I pray you never understand.

There are memories woven into my mind
that I hope you cannot wrap your head around,
years of fears and failures littering my past
that I hope you cannot fathom

I've nearly drowned in waters that I pray you've never felt,
let alone felt fill your lungs
I've left a trail of footprints through places so low, so desolate,
that I cannot bear the thought of you ever having been there yourself

I am the survivor of a thousand cuts,
the depths of which you've only scratched the surface
I am the sum of a thousand layers,
a collection of creases and crevices
that you will never truly know me until you've seen

And in time, I will let you see them.

But as long as you look,
as diligently as you study the stories
that shaped the girl who stands before you now,
as carefully as you run your finger
down the spine that binds these pages you've yet to read,
as fully as you come to know
the history that keeps me going just as it keeps me up at night,
the battles that inspire my nightmares and my dreams alike,

I love you enough to pray you never understand.

It's dizzying, isn't it,

to be so delicately imbalanced-

to feel everything fully,

right down to the weight of feeling nothing at all.

It's such a fine line between flying and falling, isn't it?

Between daydreaming and sleepwalking,
optimism and escapism,
reveling and unraveling

It's dizzying, isn't it,

To be so delicately imbalanced–
to feel everything fully,
right down to the weight of feeling nothing at all

To ricochet between righting wrongs and riding highs,
quiet cataclysms and amplified emotions,
love too loud to contain and pain too deep to unpocket

To spend half your days staring at the sun,
the other half praying for shade,
half chasing storms and half dodging raindrops;
half racing the wind, half bracing for crash landings,
hiding bruises and breeze-burns under hell-bent wings

It's exhausting, isn't it,

> To have days of smooth sailing,
> days you wouldn't know you'd moved at all
> if not for the whiplash

> To be a flower on the wall and an elephant in the room,
> a life on the eye of a needle:
> to glance is to miss it completely,
> to look too closely is more risk than it's worth

> To build for days only to fold in seconds,
> bruising before you bend, bending before you break,
> mending each time with thicker skin and a thinner frame,
> terrified that you grew up far too quickly-
> *terrified that you never will.*

It's frightening, isn't it,

> To look down and see how far you've come,
> how far you've got to fall

> To wonder if the fear of gravity is ever really outgrown,
> if one day it'll fuel your flight or anchor all your highest hopes

> To fly, and fall, and fall and fly,
> **and finally lose sight of any distinction at all between the two.**

It's such a fine line,

> *isn't it?*

Is this what you wanted?

Are you still sentient as you were when you chose this course,
or do you find yourself stumbling for the numbness in your feet?

Have you forgotten how to wield the *what ifs* in your favor?
is *fulfilled* no more than myth and hearsay, a wanderer's mirage?

Do your best laid plans and plans laid waste
resonate with the hope you held?
Do you still hold it?

Are the routines turned refuge more safety or shackles,
the dreams you had hallowed or hollow?

Are you content or complacent, these days?

Would you even know the difference?

Oh how the might-be's fall-

And I did, didn't I?

Dashed ahead of the curve into a dead-end street,
left a gaping hole where I *could've-would've-should've* been,
carried the remains of every someday goal gone cold.

It's crushing, truly:
crash-landing on the latter of to be or not to be,
watching long-held reveries resign to latency and gravestone.

Because potential starts to scream when left unsung,
and lives un-lived are a haunting thing.

I suppose by now I've given up the ghosts.

Because I've outgrown the handprints in the concrete path I poured,
traced the map lines to more understated ends
I heard a softer calling, miles beyond my best laid plans,
saw the heights I'd ached to reach were set on someone else's ladder.

Truth be told, *I have no interest in a life of constant climbing*
after empty accolades and borrowed daydreams.

The bravest thing I ever did was let go of the rungs.

And
    fall.

They ask if I've any plans for the weekend
and I tell them *I'm going home,*
cross state lines to my parents' house,
tell them the very same when I pack up to leave.

And I don't know when I came to believe it:

> That *home* is wherever I'm not.
> That it's only freedom if I'm on the way out.
> That, one of these days, *I'll finally find a way to leave me behind.*

Just once,

> *I'd like to like to stay.*

I guess as far as grace goes,
mine's more river than road-

Perpetually outbound, ever unmoored,
never round-trip and never at bay
I raise every sail and I sever the anchor,
bind my heart to the mast and cast off,
burn the atlas and snuff out the lighthouse

I send my love one way, signed and sealed,
delivered same-day free of charge
I forgive, and forget the return address,
forgo the apologies I never got
and lie awake with those I never got to give

I hoard the blame I can't bear to pass,
grit my teeth under weight I can't shed,
all the long while wearing out the word *fine*
right along with my heart and my soles

I know mercy by name till I hear it call mine,
push for balance till I'm the one losing it
I'm aware of my worth till the time comes to pay it,
proffer patience until I'm in need,
put compassion on a pedestal only I cannot climb

Because as far as grace goes,
mine's more river than road-

   It goes,
     and it goes,
       and it goes.

And should you ever want to know me,
ask me of the lengths I've gone to,
the fires I've set,
all to know the sunshine of a spotless mind.

All to find
that to be spotless
is to be empty, colorless, complacent.

Ask me if it was worth it.

Not all that much better, no, but I-

For a moment, saw the waking nightmare part into a daydream,
and it felt like premonition, like a promise /
Made plans and then showed up- more than showed up, I was *there*,
went to lunch with Mom and ordered what I wanted

Spent time sitting with the dissonance and deconstructing rhythms,
untangling chords from piles at my feet /
Listening to this body and this diamond mind of mine,
allowing them to rest, to feel, to eat

Finally asked for help- in just a whisper, barely there-
and by happenstance an angel on Earth heard it /
Slowed down for a second, minute, hour, for a day,
and didn't listen when I said I hadn't earned it

Saw the pitch black start to ease into a darkness I can see in,
enough to spot the switch still out of reach /
Enough to be reminded that there's *so much more than this*,
that there's a light and life ahead I've yet to see

Let my skin and heart and soul run free and breathe a little while,
faced the wind and sun and rain, some hard truths too /
Answered honestly and told them that I'm *not all that much better*,
but I sorta think I will be someday soon.

I really think I will be someday soon.

I will learn
to love this body
for the sake
of the soul it carries

and it will outshine
the love stories
of even my wildest
teenage dreams

- That is a *promise*.

Today
I looked down
and saw more of me
than I used to

and I thought,
with not an ounce of pretense,
not a moment's hesitation:
"I'm getting stronger."

I must be getting stronger.

I am not a body, not an aesthetic,
certainly not a mistake.

I am neither a pretty face, nor a flawed one.

I am not the sum of my skin and bones,
of my blood and muscle.

I am a *survivor*.

And for the first time in a long time,
I will feel as alive as I look.

My face will be fuller
but the smile that fills it will be real

My stomach will fold
in ways it never used to,
my body move in places it never did
but what's inside will be protected, safe

I'll be freer than I've ever been
and some will look at me and say
she's really let herself go

And I'll be beaming, saying finally,

finally,

finally.

And if ever I begin to hate
this body that carries me today,

may I never forget just how much it's carried me through.

Today I looked in the mirror
and was not inclined to like
the form reflected there-
but I loved her anyway.

She has survived so much, after all,
what does any of it matter:
the way the light decides to refract from her skin,
the shape and the size of her shadow?

She *survived.*

But they say that nothing changes if nothing changes,
so you *change*.

You change your hair- a few inches gone, a few more, then *you know what?*
Just go ahead and chop it. You change the route you take to work, and when
that isn't enough, you change work itself, put in a few weeks' notice and
slam that laptop shut for the last time, all to open a new one a few weeks
later. You change cities, pack up your apartment in a matter of a day, spend
the next hauling your life down I-75. You change gyms and change gro-
cery stores, surroundings and social scenes. You change your style too, start
wearing colors you've never much cared for- reds and browns, burnt orange
and beige, tear the closet apart and take it all to consignment. You change
your title to dog mom, buy the puppy you always wanted, change your bud-
get and routine to make room, to make a home. You change your signature
necklace and your signature scent, change phones and change out the con-
tacts, total the car you've driven since you were sixteen years old, go on and
change that too. You change your profile picture and playlists, your cosmet-
ics and your skincare, your manicures, your movement, your mantras. You
change your feed and your following, your dating app bio, exchange your
morning brew for matcha, your old laptop for a Mac.

Because they say that nothing changes if nothing changes, and at some point
you woke up and decided *you would either escape this life closing in on you or
die trying*, so you change your hair and your job, your aesthetic and city, your
people and places and habits, you buy the dog and you wear the red and you
bring home the new phone in the new car, you take the vitamins and do
the yoga, listen to the podcasts and light the candles and take the flame to
everything you've ever had or held, to all you've ever known, and it **still isn't
enough**, still doesn't make it okay, because it still isn't freedom, *it's all just
extra square footage in a brand new cage.*

Because, as you come to find out,
nothing changes if *you* don't.

So you *change*.

Today, I am grateful for those who have seen
something in me that I could not see in myself,
even more so for those who spoke it aloud-

I am grateful for those who have reminded me that the way I feel,
especially on my worst days,
is a sorely incomplete picture of the way I am,
that the way I see myself through my own lens is, at best,
a loose representation
of the mosaic of a person that is me.

Because the reality is that I want nothing more
than to bring light into others lives,
even when- especially when- I cannot see it myself,
to scatter gold onto the mundane
and thread silver linings around the dreary and disheartening

And the reality is that I have rarely, if ever, allowed myself
to consider the possibility that maybe,
in the times when I remain open enough
for the truest version of me shine through,

to those who are really paying attention,

I actually do.

It is years ago, and I am listening to my father sing me a song he wrote-

We are wired the same, he and I: regarding music as a love language, lyrics as profound conversation wrapped in the dialect of a melody. I am settled into a raggedy basement sofa, watching through welling sentimental tears as he sings about someone I used to be, someone sweet and scarless, carefree as only a toddler can be-
she wore yellow today.

It is months ago, and I feel weightless-

I am wrapped in the arms of a boy who I am still convinced must be a mirage- a boy with roots in one of my hometowns, one who's as effortless and as free-flowing as my life was when I lived there. I am enveloped in his sweatshirt- heather gray cotton, marked with the logo of a team I never liked until now- sitting in silent appreciation as the television light illuminates the bluest eyes I've ever seen, now looking back at me from beneath enviously long lashes. I am reaching for another piece of candy when he tells me that I remind him of a song-
and it was called Yellow.

It is days ago, and I am happy-

For three weeks, I have neither seen nor felt light, but the sun came up today, and it's shining on me in a way that seems to promise it will be back again, if not tomorrow, then soon. I am shopping, aimless and carefree, with a friend- the kind you feel lucky to have, a sweet soul that sees the good in the bad and shines in the way only the most authentic gems can. I am perusing the candle section, admiring my freshly painted nails- bubblegum pink- and taking in the scent of sandalwood and musk, when she pulls another candle off the shelf-
I think, if you were a color, you'd be this one- yellow is just so bright and happy.

It is hours ago, and I am thinking about how even the simplest of motifs can paint an entire story in a new light-

Because I have never liked yellow. More than that, it is entirely incongruous with the way I see myself- I am no longer an innocent toddler, dirtying her yellow dress in a sandbox while dreaming idly of castles and glass slippers; I do not believe that the stars shine for me like they do for the muse of a love song, and these days I feel like a raincloud, at times too heavy to hold my own weight, far more often than I feel like a personification of sunshine, of brightness, of cheer.

But lately, I am beginning to consider the possibility that the way I feel is a sorely incomplete picture of the way I am- that the way I see myself through my own lens is, at best, a loose representation of the mosaic of a person that is me.

Because the reality is that I want nothing more than to bring light into others lives, even when- especially when- I cannot see it myself, to scatter gold onto the mundane and thread silver linings around the dreary and disheartening.

And the reality is that I have never really allowed myself to consider the possibility that maybe, in the times when I remain open enough for the truest version of me shine through, to those who are really paying attention- *I actually do.*

It is now. The sun came up again just as it promised.

And I wore yellow today.

Because I can promise you this:
what is coming is better than what you lost.

Yes, even you.

Even now.

Kelsey Kasischke

VERITY

Let me ask you something-

    What would you do right now
       if fear didn't have any say in the matter?

        Where would you be right now
           if you really believed you were free?

Let me tell you something-

It doesn't.

And you are.

Maybe no one will understand, *and maybe that's the point.*

Maybe no one will *get it.* This thing that sets your soul ablaze, that shatters the monotonous and the mundane and makes you think this, *this*, is why I'm here. Or maybe "it" is something more understated, more inconspicuous: a joke that nearly cracks your ribcage for which any of the more *poised* people you know wouldn't have even cracked a smile, a wave or a kind word you feel undeniably called to give to a complete stranger who looks as though they could use a lifeline, however random the source. Perhaps "it" is even more personal than that: a pivot or a breakthrough, a much-needed change that, from the outside, could be sorely misinterpreted as crazy, as laziness, as self-indulgence or misdirection. Whatever "it" is, the point is this: I cannot promise that a single person besides yourself will understand, will *get it*. What I *can* promise is that **you don't need them to.**

Let them misunderstand. Let them wonder. Let them look at you sideways and turn up their noses while you throw yourself into a life much fuller, much deeper, than any they'll ever live by sticking to the mainstream. Because the worst possible outcome is not, despite what your fears tell you, you straying from the path, deviating from the pack, being different, turning everyone's expectations, including your own, upside down; the worst possible outcome is you letting those fears dim your light and diminish your life until you look and walk and talk just like the rest, just like you feel like you *should*. The worst possible outcome is you being one among the crowd-pleasers, the carbon-copies, the cookie-cutters whose truest selves are buried under layers of conformity and questions of *"but what would they think?"*

Stop asking what they were expecting from you. Stop asking what *you* were expecting from you. Start asking what you want, what you need, what you know, what you feel. Start asking who you would be if no one else had a say in the matter, **and then be them.** *Because no one else has a say in the matter.*

Maybe no one will understand. Maybe, at least at first, you won't either.

Maybe that's the point.

What if I told you that it's all still true?

That your stride through the door
still sets rooms aglow,
that electricity lives in iris and aura
even now

That the rutilant youth you so miss
never left you at all;
rather,
it courses through your veins still today,
a live wire in wait,
dances along your fingertips
and sheds light on all you touch,
lingers like a luminous imprint
wherever you walk

Your eyes have adjusted to your own light,
baby girl-

You're no less brilliant than you've ever been.

It may have to be drastic.

It may ask you to give everything you have, and then some.

It may ask you to change your very identity, your very being, every instinct and habit and aspect of the *self* you know, may ask you to rewire and reinvent every default you've come to rely on.

It may look extreme, may look senseless, may look like radical change to those who do not know the cost of staying the same, who have not had to pay the price of standing still in the places you've been. It may look like regression, look like indulgence, may feel counter-intuitive and counter-productive, counter-cultural and just plain *wrong*.

It may be the hardest thing you've ever had to do, but little by little, bit by bit, at long last, you will learn to give yourself what you need, learn to love your body for the sake of the soul it carries, learn to supply what you've denied yourself for so long: safety in your own skin.

And getting there?

It may have to be drastic.

Do this for me, darling,
before you go on praying to forget
the toll it took, the time it stole,
your weathered tread and
worn down mind -

Remember the road.

Commemorate the miles,
count every last one as victory
no matter the ones yet untraveled

Do not wipe the stories away
before you make it back home,
even the ones you can't quite tell
even still, even now

Do this for me,
before you wish it all away:

Remember the road,
remember it all,
give it as many glances
as you'd like.

Let it remind you why you're never going back.

May this be the year you find beauty in the duality of it all.

The year you lean into the essentiality of the lows
as you do the euphoria of the highs,
learn to appreciate ease and effort alike

The year you tread beaten paths and forge new ones,
find your fire and protect your peace;
the year you speak up and listen,
enlighten and learn,
earn and accept,
release and restore

May this be the year you leave nothing on the table:
not a silent win uncelebrated,
not a single loss wasted,
not a stone nor a page unturned
in the story you'll have lived come December.

May it be a story you're proud to tell.

Then you look back
on all of the tiny miracles
and bite-sized breakthroughs
that brought you here
and you realize
you never needed newsworthy,
much less grandiose -

You only needed to *notice*.

I think forgiveness is the most beautiful thing in the world.

I think there is something profound about the ability
to look into the eyes of someone who hurt you and say,
you are more than what you've done to me.

-Remember that the eyes in the mirror belong to someone too.

It is not about being your old self again,
nor is it about becoming the future self
that your old self always dreamed you would be-

It is about being who you are *now*,
knowing what you know
and having what you have

and becoming who you want to be *now*,
having been who you've been
and grown how you've grown.

Please, do not waste the lessons you've learned
and the pain that shaped you, strengthened you,
by striving to return to a previous version of yourself-

That version of you didn't know what you know,
could never tell the story that is now yours to tell.

And that is a source of strength all its own:

    that the only person who can tell it,

      is you.

Your story is more than just a bridge between your past and present—
it is a message with the power to change someone else's future,
and you are the only one who can tell it.

So tell it.

You'll wade through hell and high water on that highway to Heaven,
you'll scrap for every ounce of silver in your lining

Those sleepless nights and starry eyes
are only side effects of dreaming-

It's the ebb and flow, the patience and the pining

That's the thing about being someone who stays-

You will have to lose what God knows you would never release.

You are so prone to seeing the good in people, so prone to having faith that they just need more time, more patience, more love, that it will often take something being ripped from your hands before you will let it go, no matter how heavy it becomes.

So you will lose.

You will lose time and time again- sometimes without explanation, sometimes with such searing pain that you'll the thought of starting again will paralyze you with fear, sometimes leaving you so utterly empty-handed that you'll have a hard time believing that anything will ever be yours to keep.

Until it is.

And that's when you'll realize that the heart that made all the lesser loves so hard to let go of is the same one that will make the real thing thrive.

Because eventually you'll find that you were never being punished for always being the one to stay longer, love harder, give more-
you were being guided to the one who will do the same for you.

Eventually, you'll see that you were never being told no-

You were being told *not yet.*

And may these be my intentions
today and every day:

To leave people better than I find them,
and to be left better than I am found.

If tonight I lay my head to rest
having done nothing else,

I will have done well.

But actually it's all symbolic and it *is* that deep, if you think about it.

And I'm thinking about it. The way they carry cars by truck down the interstate, lest the tires learn to love the open road too soon, and I keep a perfectly good heart in hiding. The way I was born on Central time and live on Eastern, and perhaps that's why I'm perpetually ahead of myself these days. The way one of my childhood dogs died of cancer and the other died that night of a broken heart, and I never understood it until mine took a beating, took a break from beating, two Octobers ago. The way he liked my hair long and the number eleven, so I lost eleven inches and the weight of the world. The way we run away only to find our way back to the places we felt most free, to the people who feel like home. The way we cut up fruit for the people we love, carry their baggage, *here let me get that for you*, help them lay down whatever's heavy. The way we still reference that line from that movie that we watched with a best friend we haven't seen in God knows how long, still use that phrase we picked up from a long-gone love, still brew our tea the way that one barista swore was best, still feel twenty-two every time we drive through the Bluegrass, still hear that song and wonder who he is nowadays, how he's been since leaving that college town. The way we bookmark the dates and places that left us scarred and revisit them years later to rewrite the narrative, to shed a lighter kind of tears, to bloom where we've bled. The way I told him he'd read my writing when I was dead and buried, and now that *me too* from a kindred reader is what reminds me why I'm still alive.

Because it's all symbolic and it *is* that deep, and if some aspect of the ordinary makes your life a little less ordinary, if something light as a feather strikes you in just the right way to move you, to change your mind, to make you pick up the phone or smile at the sky or cry on a shoulder-

Let it.

Here's the thing:
Your mistakes are already accounted for in the plan for your life.

It's often said that what is coming is better than what was lost, and this is absolutely true- but what's also true, and what's harder to really believe, is that what's coming is better than what was lost *even if it's your fault that you lost it.*

It's easy to let guilt convince you that you missed your chance, that you blew it, that you couldn't possibly have something better on the way if you couldn't even manage to hold onto the good things that you've already had; it's easy to buy into the lie that it's on you to correct every mistake, reverse every consequence, regain every loss in order to get your life "back on track".

But maybe it's time to consider that nothing you've done ever had the power steer it off track in the first place.

Maybe it's time to consider that your failures, from the minor slip-ups to the most crushing mistakes you've ever made, are not only part of the plan, *they are essential to it.*

That opportunity you threw away, that heart you broke, that thing or person or part of yourself that you lost, was never meant to hang over your head, and was certainly never meant to be something that you spend your life trying to earn back-

It was intentionally placed in your life knowing that you will make mistakes, knowing that you will have to lose a few battles in order to be prepared to win the ones that really matter.

It hurts because it *has to.*

It hurts because you wouldn't do anything differently next time if it *didn't.*

So give sincere apologies, do what you can to heal the pain you caused, spend enough time turning the loss over in your hands to learn the weight of it and memorize it's edges, then *put it down.*

Put it down and forgive yourself. Even before you see the better thing come along, even before you find out when or how you're going to need the lesson the loss was meant to teach or the purpose it was meant to serve, *even before the other people involved have forgiven you.*

**Because you had to mess up that good thing
to learn how not to mess up *the* good thing.**

Because the greater plan for your life isn't contingent on your ability to put the pieces back together or scratch and claw your way back to where you were before the fallout- *so your plan shouldn't be either.*

Because I can promise you this:
what is coming is better than what you lost.

Yes, even you.

Even now.

Because that's the thing about hope:
   it's never really gone when it goes.

   And here you are,
      hoping that's true.

      Almost like it never left at all.

That's the thing about hope:
it does not move in silence.

It's such quiet company,
a commotion on its way
indiscreet in motion,
inconspicuous in the meantime,
as loud on arrival as it is in abandon

It goes unnoticed,
never leaves that way
returns unexpectedly,
never unannounced,
blends in till its impolite exit,
floods back like first light on a dark age

You'll forget it's there
until it slams the door,
forget its face
until it comes back knocking,
forget all too easily in its absence
that although the feeling flickers,
the fuel's in endless supply

Because the thing about hope
is that it's never really gone when it goes.

And here you are,
hoping that's true.

Must be closer than you think.

What if you, I don't know, sent the text?

Or dialed the number, made the call, hell, dropped the phone and put rubber to pavement? What if you stopped ruminating on all of this untold truth and said what needed to be said, stopped trying so hard to anticipate the way the words would land and just took the leap? *Because you're suffocating, right?* You're a prisoner to this love you insist on holding hostage, will be until you give it somewhere to go, and you're trying so very hard to keep it from the only one for whom it lights up like a damn supernova. There is a person who holds a little piece of you on the other end of that line, the other end of that street, and there are a million and one ways your life could end tomorrow, tonight, the minute you finish reading what I'm about to tell you, so *hear me while you have the chance:* the love is either worth the risk, **or it is not love at all.** Truly. If the one on your mind is not worth the shaking hands, the broken voice, the ineloquent words and flushed face of a courageous mess who doesn't know what they're saying but only knows it needs to be said, then **there's nothing to be said at all.** It terrifies you because it *matters.* It terrifies you because it's moments like these that tether you to this life we're living, that fill you with purpose to the point of boiling over, that remind you why we're here on this beautifully petrifying floating rock in the first place. It terrifies you because it's love, would be love, could be love, and there is no love without choice, and choice means that no one can guarantee you will be chosen in return, but *God,* if you love them, even think you *could* love them, is it really the worst thing for them to know that you believe them to be worth choosing? To hear it from you? And if it turns out to be unreciprocated, is it the worst thing for you to find out in this way that there is another love out there you've yet to find, one that's meant to be yours, one that will choose you too? And if it *is* reciprocated- what if it *is? Do you not want, not need, to find out?* Because it will kill you to go on wondering, right? *Because you're suffocating, aren't you?* Because you're the warden and prisoner alike to this love that you insist on holding hostage, will be until you give it permission to go where it wants to go, and *neither of you will ever walk free if you don't open that door.* So, hear me out-

What if you, I don't know,

opened that door?

I have built enough houses on shifting sand
to know that talk is cheap
and intentions are far more important than interest.

Anyone can want you, darling-
find someone who *wants to be with you.*

-The former will let you know it;

the latter will never let you doubt it.

What a tragedy it would be,
what a perversion of truth,
to go on believing that love is cruel
when love has been the only antidote to cruelty all along

Of all the lies
you have been led to believe,
may you never believe
that love is cruel-

The Sun is steadfast, essential,
immensely powerful,
but you would never know it
had you only ever sought its evidence
from a distant, shifting, waning moon
with a limited capacity to reflect it.

Love is steadfast, essential,
immensely powerful,
patient and kind and secure;
never think it any less so
based on another human being's
limited capacity to reflect it.

*-The light of the moon
was never meant to be enough.*

So you go back.

Or, rather, you let them come back. Either way, you're back to where you started, where you swore you'd never be again, with the very person you fought so hard to forget. **And at first it feels like coming home, doesn't it?**

At first it's more a relief than a relapse, more an exhale than a held breath. And that almost makes you believe that this is where you belong, have always belonged, always will. But the thing is, once the transient illusion inevitably fades, you will be reminded of precisely why you had to leave the last time, and the time before that, and the time before that. Once the golden glow of the reunion wears off, the graytone of reality sets in, and **it is just as dark as you've tried so hard not to remember it.** And still you think *it must be love*, because you cannot, for the life of you, let it go, but it's not love, no, **it's the illusion of control.** Because if you go in knowing you're going to get hurt, you remove the ambiguity that comes with allowing yourself to hope for something better. Because high hopes mean the potential for letdowns, and nothing makes you feel more out of control than handing someone else the power to disappoint you, or, perhaps even more terrifying, *love you in the way that you deserve to be loved*, take your life as you know it and turn it upside down. So you cling to this familiar pain, this comfortable prison, **because the truth is that you would choose sitting in hell with the devil you know over taking flight to find out just where those wings of yours might take you.** But the devil you know isn't in your corner, certainly isn't the love of your life- **he's a predator with a silver tongue and an eye for opportunity.**

And you'd never let the words "*I deserve better*" slip from your lips, but if you're honest, deep down in some hidden part of yourself, **you know that you do.** By staying with someone who treats you poorly, though, you assuage that subconscious feeling of inadequacy that's plagued you for so long- because, whether you'd dare admit it to yourself or not, you will always have the comfort of knowing that, between the two of you, **you are the one who deserves better.** In fact, the worse it gets, the more it hurts, the more that innate feeling of unworthiness is satisfied, the more you at last find relief from that ceaseless unspoken fear of never being good enough. Because they will always give you just enough love to justify staying and just enough pain to cater to your distorted self-perception, and **you will always be the martyr willing to walk through fire to prove your love, but that isn't love, darling, it's self-destruction.** It's Stockholm syndrome. It's certainty at all costs, even the cost of your soul.

So you go back, and at first it feels like coming home, doesn't it, **until the flames begin to lick your skin once more and that sinking feeling settles into your bones.** Until it burns just enough for you to decide that you will no longer let yourself be enslaved to this insatiable craving for control, are no longer enamored with familiar toxicity or predictable pain. Until you begin to let the fear of the unknown excite rather than terrify you, at last admit to yourself that **you do not belong here, never did, never will.** Because home isn't where the hurt is, isn't where you're comfortable, *isn't even the place you know like the back of your hand.*

It's where you're *loved.*

My greatest ambitions
aren't praises or riches-

no, just to belong and be *free*.

Kelsey Kasischke

REVERIE

Give me spaces to roam
   and a face to call home,
      a safe place to fall at the day's end
A slow steady burn,
   a man of his word,
      a lover and leader and best friend

Windows-down drives,
   warm hands and kind eyes,
      bouquets without any occasion
A roof and four walls,
   little feet down the halls,
      cold coffee and good conversation

A prayer when i'm lost,
   a pen for my thoughts,
      a playlist for living room dances
Silver-lined skies,
   a sweeping sunrise,
      each week seven more second chances

My greatest ambitions
   aren't praises or riches-
      no, just to belong and be free
To plant roots and grow,
   to make haven of home-

    That's the life and the love of my dreams.

I cannot imagine a dream as sweet,
a someday as simple and celestial as this:

To find the love
who says my name
as though it were the one-word answer
to a lifetime of prayers

And sweeter still:

to be the love
who proves Heaven
heard every

       last

         one.

There will be days
when you love to choose me
and days when you love me
by choosing me regardless

Just promise me this:
that you will choose to love me
either way,
every day,
whatever that looks like.

Either way,
every day,
whatever that looks like.

It's simple, really-

Hold me and you'll never have to doubt,
see me and you'll never disappear,
learn me and you'll never go unknown

Mind me and you'll never be uncared for,
move me and I'll keep you front of mind,
protect me and you'll never need to share.

-Love me and you'll never be alone.

Do not dream of me
prim and portrait-ready, quiet and composed-

Dream of me dancing across kitchen tiles,
twirling under your arm to the rhythm of the rain,
exchanging lost hope for harmony and home

Color me in chords, paint me in playlists;
let me give life to the lyrics you adore,
be the face that fills your mind
when you hear a chorus that closes your eyes

-In a world full of noise,
    let me be music to your ears.

I do not care to be your Mona Lisa-

No, instead
cast me as the lady of your favorite love songs
let me star in the ballads that pull your lips into a smile,
your heartstrings into a forget-me-knot

Do not dream of me
prim and portrait-ready, quiet and composed-
dream of me dancing across kitchen tiles,
twirling under your arm to the rhythm of the rain,
exchanging lost hope for harmony and home

No, I do not envy da Vinci's muse
because the Louvre sounds to me like a loveless place
knowing that music has always held your heart
longer than a museum ever could

So color me in chords,
paint me in playlists;
let me give life to the lyrics you adore,
be the face that fills your mind
when you hear a chorus that closes your eyes

but *do not make me your Mona Lisa.*

Because many masterpieces have gone before me,
all of them flawless enough to catch your eye,
all of them fleeting enough to lose it

So, truth be told,
I would rather not be your *work of art.*

No, love-

Let me be music to your ears.

Hold me gently,
shatter me sweetly.

Bring diamonds to my eyes
in the way the others couldn't;
let me crumble in the palm of your hand,
and keep me contentedly there

There is beauty in remaining breakable-
even the mountains give way to the wind in time.

So let me be at once safe and sound, moved and changed,
delicate and empowered,
lest I ever go unaffected, uninspired.

Lest I ever go loveless again.

Give me a daisy on the dashboard and a diamond on my hand,

a heart to call home and a safe place to land

Ask any romantic, and they'll tell you:
There's just something about the city.

There's just something spellbinding about the skyline,
something cathartic about the passing cars and the vibrant bars,
all bustling parts of a never-moving whole

There's something captivating in the juxtaposition,
the way it courses with an energy like that between two magnets:
a state of paradoxical grace,
a delicate balance poised on the feeling
of being both fully exposed and fully invisible,
monumental and microscopic,
older and wiser and more certain than you've ever been
that certainty is an illusion you've fallen prey to for the last time, again.

Something like love, when you think about it.

Maybe it's the lovers on the levee tonight,
the lavender haze on the Ohio;
maybe it's the rosy hue of Mount Adams
blushing while the sun winks out over the horizon-

But I think God was spinning Sinatra when he strung those city lights,
think he'd just spilled tears on a poem
when he dreamt up skyscraper backdrops and riverboat rides,
think he retired his most wished-upon stars to line that horizon,
and I think it's *all so hard not to romanticize*

Because many have gone looking for love in the city,
and many more will do the same,
and God, why *wouldn't* they,
when the greatest love story yet untold
is always a sidewalk or a stoplight away.

Ask any romantic, and they'll tell you:

There's just something about it.

If I hold your hand out in the sun, our shadows follow suit-

how beautiful: the brightest loves mean sharing darkness too.

He carries my groceries and my burdens,
knows my favorite flavors and the worst of my fears

He asks because he wants to know,
never to fill the silence,
pays attention to the details
as though the reservoir will never run dry-

> *What is it about this song that you love so much?*
> *Where did you learn how to do that?*
> *What's the story behind this poem of yours?*
> *Have raspberries always been your favorite?*
> *What is it you dream about, these days?*

He stands at the stove while I weave him into poems,
tucks my hair behind my ear and hums a Sunday morning tune,
opens the window to let the sun pour in and I am light,

light,

light.

So I rest my head between his collarbone and jaw,
confess that *I can only offer him everything.*

And he wants all of it and more.

I hope you find a love:

I hope you find a love
that's both your solid ground
and your ninth cloud,
your anchor and your open sea,
right where you've always belonged
and everywhere you've never been

I hope you find a love
that learns you well,
but would never be so naïve
as to believe
that every stone
within your ever evolving,
intricate self
could be overturned
in only a lifetime

I hope you find a love
that'd sooner walk through a flame
than watch your light burn out
A love that feels for the switch
when your bright eyes dim,
fuels the hearthflame
when you wander too far,
knows where to find you
when you yourself do not

I hope you find a love
that craves your thoughts
and braves your storms,
one that doesn't shy away
from the worst of your war tales
because *therein lie the stories*
that shaped you

I hope you find a love
that is not satisfied
with taking you at face value,
one that would rather drown
in the depths beneath your surface
than stay afloat atop anyone else's

I hope you find a love
that gives flowers without reason
and reassurance without request,
one that takes its time
and takes no offense
to the walls you're still dismantling
from the ones that came before

I hope you find a love
that drinks coffee with you at 2am
fending off sleep to bask in your company,
to soak in every detail of your history
and map out every dream for the future,
to laugh about things that don't matter
with someone who does

I hope you find a love
that spins you around the kitchen
and holds back your hair,
that puts you in their playlists
and holds you as though you're
the embodied answer to a lifetime of prayers-
I hope they're the answer to every one of yours

I hope you find a love
hellbent on bringing Heaven down,
putting it in your pocket for a rainy day
A love that bears your burden
long before telling you to lighten your step,
one that does not intend to fix you-
only to point you sunward
when the shade creeps in,
only to grow as you go

I hope you find a love
devoid of doubts and second guesses
One that chooses you
with such unwavering certainty,
good and bad days alike,
that you hardly remember
they ever had any other options at all

I hope you find the love
of all your wildest dreams

and I hope it's wilder still.

I hope you find a love
that's both your solid ground
and your ninth cloud,
your anchor and your open sea,
right where you've always belonged
and everywhere you've never been

I hope you find a love
that learns you well,
but would never be so naïve
as to believe that every stone
within your ever evolving, intricate self
could be overturned in only a lifetime

I hope you find a love
that'd sooner walk through a flame
than watch your light burn out
A love that feels for the switch
when your bright eyes dim,
fuels the hearthflame
when you wander too far,
knows where to find you
when you yourself do not

I hope you find a love
that craves your thoughts
and braves your storms,
one that doesn't shy away
from the worst of your war tales
because *therein lie the stories*
that shaped you

I hope you find a love
that spins you around the kitchen
and holds back your hair,
that puts you in their playlists
and holds you as though you're
the embodied answer to a lifetime of prayers-
I hope they're the answer to every one of yours

I hope you find a love
that gives flowers without reason
and reassurance without request,
one that takes its time
and takes no offense
to the walls you're still dismantling
from the ones that came before

I hope you find a love
that drinks coffee with you at 2am
fending off sleep to bask in your company,
to soak in every detail of your history
and map out every dream for the future,
to laugh about things that don't matter
with someone who does

I hope you find a love
that is not satisfied with taking you at face value,
one that would rather drown
in the depths beneath your surface
than stay afloat atop anyone else's

I hope you find a love
hellbent on bringing Heaven down,
putting it in your pocket for a rainy day
A love that bears your burden
long before telling you to lighten your step,
one that does not intend to fix you—
only to point you sunward
when the shade creeps in,
only to grow as you go

I hope you find a love
devoid of doubts and second guesses
One that chooses you
with such unwavering certainty,
good and bad days alike,
that you hardly remember
they ever had any other options at all.

ABOUT THE AUTHOR

Kelsey Kasischke is a 26-year-old independent author living in Atlanta, Georgia with her dog Yogi. *I Can Only Offer You Everything* is the second book she's published, the first being another book of poetry and prose titled *Indigo Flame*.

Her social media handles for writing purposes are *@writtenbykelseyk*; be sure to follow for new content, updates on future publications, and/or to say hello and let her know what you thought of *I Can Only Offer You Everything*.

Lastly, she appreciates each and every one of her readers for lending their time and attention to her words. Being able to share her writing in this way is a dream come true, and to have people like you read and appreciate her work is an honor that she will never take for granted. She is incredibly excited for what's to come, and hopes you are as well.

I Can Only Offer You Everything